AESOP'S FABLES

ILLUSTRATED BY
HEIDI HOLDER

MACMILLAN CHILDREN'S BOOKS

To Friends of Animals, Inc.
and to Friends of the Earth

H. H.

Illustrations copyright © Heidi Holder 1981
Text copyright © Viking Penguin Inc 1981
This version copyright © Macmillan Publishers Ltd 1981

First published 1981 by
MACMILLAN CHILDREN'S BOOKS
A division of Macmillan Publishers Limited
London and Basingstoke
Associated companies throughout the world

Picturemac edition published 1988

British Library Cataloguing in Publication Data
Aesop
 [Fables. *English. Selections*] Aesop's fables.
 I. Title   II. Holder, Heidi
 888'.0108   PZ8.2

ISBN 0-333-37145-3

Printed in Hong Kong

Note: the text of this edition of the *Fables* has been adapted by
the publishers from several sources – primarily the versions by
Boris Artzybasheff and Sir Roger L'Estrange.

CONTENTS

AESOP'S FABLES

THE DOVE AND THE SNAKE

One day a beautiful Dove was preening her feathers when she saw the Snake hiding in the bushes. As she watched the Snake, she did not see a Hunter stalking her with his net. Closer and closer he came, but still the Dove did not see him. Suddenly, the Snake slithered out of his hiding place and the Hunter was so startled that he dropped his net. In the confusion that followed, the Dove quickly flew away to safety.

Good may come out of evil, and even our worst enemies may help us without meaning to.

THE TOWN MOUSE AND
THE COUNTRY MOUSE

A Town Mouse once went to visit her cousin in the country. The Country Mouse was an honest, generous creature and she wanted to make her cousin feel welcome. She looked in her store cupboard and took out all that she found there—peas, and barley, and nuts and little scraps of cheese. It was not a rich feast, for the Country Mouse lived a poor and simple life, but she put the food in front of her friend and did not eat anything herself so that the Town Mouse should have plenty.

But the Town Mouse was not used to such simple country meals and she wrinkled up her nose and picked here and there at the food. At last she said to her cousin, "My dear, I must be honest with you. I just don't know how you can stand this dull country life with nothing but woods and meadows all round you and little but peas and barley to eat. Come with me to the town where there are busy streets full of people! Don't you long to live in luxury and dine on fine foods? I promise you, life in the town is much better than this."

The Country Mouse was persuaded by the fine words of her friend, and she agreed to set off for the town right away. When they arrived, the Town Mouse took her to the great mansion where she lived. It was richer and grander than anything the Country Mouse had imagined. There were soft velvet couches, ivory carvings and beautiful Persian carpets, and on the table stood the remains of a splendid banquet. Now it was the turn of the Town Mouse to play hostess. She

ran to and fro fetching everything her guest could wish and serving her dish after dish of the most dainty and delicious food.

The Country Mouse sat and enjoyed herself, delighted by everything around her. She thought of her home in the country, and she saw that it was indeed a poor and miserable life she had led there. But, at that moment, they heard growling and barking.

"What is that?" said the Country Mouse.

"It is only the dogs of the house," answered the other.

"Only!" said the Country Mouse. "I do not like that music at my dinner."

Just at that moment the door flew open, in came two huge mastiffs, and the two mice scampered off as fast as they could go.

"Good-bye, dear cousin," said the Country Mouse.

"What! Going so soon?" said the other.

"Yes," she replied—

"Better peas and barley in peace than cakes and jelly in fear."

THE BAT, THE BRAMBLEBUSH,
AND THE CORMORANT

A Bat, a Bramblebush, and a Cormorant decided to set up in business together. The Bat borrowed money to help the business, the Bramblebush bought some cloth, and the Cormorant brought some brass coins. The three of them sailed across the sea to sell their goods, but their ship ran into a great storm and capsized. The three merchants escaped unhurt, but all their goods were lost.

Ever since, the Bat never goes out before dark because he is afraid of meeting people to whom he owes money. The Bramblebush is forever catching at the clothes of passersby in the hope it will find its own cloth again. And the Cormorant always hovers over the coast, searching for brass coins washed ashore by the tide.

Those who have suffered a great misfortune will remember it for ever.

THE HORSE AND
THE LADEN ASS

Horse and an Ass were travelling together on a long journey with their master. The Horse had no load to carry, but the Ass was weighed down with many heavy bundles.

Staggering under the weight, the Ass cried out to the Horse: "Please, good Sir, please help me to carry my load, or I am afraid I shall die."

But the proud Horse did not care about the Ass's suffering and refused to help.

Soon the little Ass was exhausted and, stumbling, the poor animal fell down. No matter how hard he tried he could not get back on to his feet again. Seeing this, their master lifted all the bundles off the Ass's back and flung them across the back of the Horse, who at once began to moan and groan and wail.

"What a miserable creature I am!" he cried. "What suffering I have brought upon myself! I refused to carry a share of the load, and look what has happened to me: now I have to carry it all by myself!"

The strong should help the weak, as this will make life easier for both of them.

THE FOX AND THE GRAPES

There was a hungry Fox went out looking for food. But he could not find anything to eat and his hunger grew and grew. Then, as he walked through an orchard, he saw a bunch of delicious ripe grapes hanging high above his head. The Fox licked his lips and decided the grapes would make a tasty meal. So he took a run and a jump and leaped at the grapes. But he could not reach them. Turning round again with a One, Two, Three, he jumped up once more, but still he could not reach them. Again and again he tried, until at last he gave up. Weary, and very hungry, he turned and trotted away with his nose in the air, saying to himself, "Those grapes were sour anyway!"

It is easy to despise what you cannot get.

THE MARRIAGE OF THE SUN

Many years ago, during a very hot summer, it was said that the Sun was going to be married. All the birds and the beasts were delighted at the prospect of the wedding and they began to prepare for a great celebration.

The Frogs, in particular, were determined to honour the occasion. Dressed in their finest clothes, they were preparing a festival of singing and dancing, when a wise old Toad spoke to them.

"My friends," he said, "it would be a good idea if you were all a little less excited, for this marriage might bring us more sorrow than joy. Just think, if one hot Sun can dry up the wet marshes so that we can hardly bear it, what will happen to us if there should be half a dozen baby Suns as well?"

It is possible to have too much of a good thing.

THE COCK AND THE JEWEL

A fine young Cock was scratching about in the farmyard looking for something to eat when he found a shining jewel lying in the straw. It sparkled brilliantly, but the Cock shrugged and shook his head, saying: "You may be a treasure to a man but you are no use to me. I would rather have a few grains of corn than all the jewels in the world."

What is valuable to some may be worthless to others.

THE HARE AND THE TORTOISE

Hare was once boasting to the other animals about how fast he could run.

"I challenge any one of you to a race," he said.

The Tortoise said quietly: "I accept your challenge."

The Hare thought this was a good joke. "I could dance round you all the way," he said.

"Keep your boasting until you've won the race," said the Tortoise. "Shall we begin?"

At once the Hare ran off out of sight. He was sure he would win and to show his contempt for the Tortoise he lay down to have a nap. He was soon sound asleep.

Meanwhile, the Tortoise plodded on and on, and when the Hare awoke he saw the Tortoise almost at the winning post. The Hare leaped up, but it was too late. The Tortoise had won. Then the Tortoise turned to the Hare and said:

"It is better to work slowly and steadily than to have great talents and waste them."

THE STAG AT THE POOL

Stag came to a pool to drink. As he bent over the water he caught sight of his own reflection.

"Ah," he said proudly, "what beautiful antlers I have! But what a pity my legs are so thin and spindly. I would rather have no legs at all than those bony things!"

At that moment the Stag heard the sound of huntsmen and their hounds. Alarmed, he raced away and soon left his pursuers behind. But, as he ran through some bushes, his antlers caught in the branches. He struggled to get free as the baying of the hounds grew nearer. At last the Stag said to himself, "If I am meant to be killed by those beasts, I should at least face them calmly." As he said this he stopped struggling and his antlers became free.

At once he bounced off again, his long thin legs carrying him quickly and safely from danger. As he ran he thought, "How lucky I am! And how foolish I was before! My antlers, which I was so proud of, nearly brought me to my death, but my legs, which I despised, have saved me!"

What is worth most is often valued least.